Little Black Box

Little Black Box

Speculative Poetry from Ohio

Edited by
Anna Cates

RESOURCE *Publications* · Eugene, Oregon

LITTLE BLACK BOX
Speculative Poetry from Ohio

Copyright © 2023 Wipf and Stock Publishers. All rights reserved. Except for brief quotations in critical publications or reviews, no part of this book may be reproduced in any manner without prior written permission from the publisher. Write: Permissions, Wipf and Stock Publishers, 199 W. 8th Ave., Suite 3, Eugene, OR 97401.

Resource Publications
An Imprint of Wipf and Stock Publishers
199 W. 8th Ave., Suite 3
Eugene, OR 97401

www.wipfandstock.com

PAPERBACK ISBN: 978-1-6667-6438-3
HARDCOVER ISBN: 978-1-6667-6439-0
EBOOK ISBN: 978-1-6667-6440-6

07/11/23

For all who wander but are not lost

May the wind under your wings bear you
where the sun sails and the moon walks.

—J. R. R. TOLKIEN

Contents

Acknowledgments | xi
Introduction | xv

KATHY B. AUSTIN
    Afterimage | 1
    Happiness | 2
    Grief at the Window | 3
    Ohio the Eve of Invasion | 4
    Where Will the Blue Mole Skink Live? | 5

STEVE BROIDY
    Galadriel's Mirror | 6
    Toward a Poetic of Space Travel | 7
    The Ram's Tale | 8
    Last Light | 10
    Vacuity | 11
    Ghosts and Where to Find Them | 12

ANNA CATES
    Little Black Box | 13
    Three Triolets | 14
    The Golem & the Nazi | 16
    Orc | 17

    The Final Fairy | 18
    Alice | 19

LINDA Z. CHERNICK
    Autumn Monoku | 20
    Evil Wind | 21

ED DAVIS
    Two Gods | 22
    Epitaph | 23
    Crows | 24

CATHRYN ESSINGER
    What The Black Cat Is Not | 25
    For Six Friends | 26
    Half in Love | 27
    The Map Makers | 28
    Rumors of War | 29
    Dark Matter | 30

SHARON H. FROST
    spirit of the woods | 31
    midsummer | 31
    glowing moon | 31
    Crime-Ku | 32
    Escape into Obliteration | 33

Contents

Autumn Tanka | 34
*by Sharon H. Frost
and Anna Cates*

DAVID LEE GARRISON
Sweeping the Cemetery | 35
And Dog Said | 36
Daphne to Apollo | 37
Salmacis | 38
Infinity | 39

PATRICK S. GENTILE
Boanerges | 40
Lush Sicilian Girls | 41

JENNIFER HAMBRICK
the little girl stopped | 42
in the rampant twilight | 43
Morning Zoo | 44
Memory | 45
The Open Box | 46

ARTIE ISAAC
Poem to My Ghost | 47
*by Artie Isaac and
Sharon H. Frost*

FREDERIC STUART (SKIP) LEEDS
Fahrenheit 01C3 | 48
Crusader | 49
I Advance to Game | 51
The World Is Spinning | 52
Dire Moth | 53
Star Trek Liberal | 55

S. MIA LING
. . . and if a ghost should
meet a ghost . . . | 58
Effluvia | 59
A Photograph of the Painter
Painting the Two Fridas | 61
Persephone and the
Girls Club | 64
The Love We Bore Him, Elegy
to Conrad Balliet | 66

HERBERT WOODWARD MARTIN
A Monk's Prayer and
Blessing | 68

JULIE L. MOORE
Opening Day | 69
Shadow of Death | 71
Aftershock | 72
In a parallel universe | 74
The first time I saw a
shooting star | 75
Prufrock in My Backyard | 76

ROBERT PASCHELL
If the Sun Is a White Witch | 77
Archaeopteryx | 78
Untitled | 79
The Hidden Valley | 80

DAVID A. PETREMAN
What To Do With a
Dead Angel | 81

Contents

Valentina Ranaldi-Adams
Proxima b citizens | 82
two hearts | 82
moon walk | 82
I have the legs | 82
streaming now | 82
black widow spider | 82

Janeal Turnbull Ravndal
All Things New | 83
Meeting for Worship | 84
Visitor | 85

Barbara A. Sabol
cocooned | 86
immense heaven | 86
red moon | 86
planetarium | 86
Field Notes from the Moons of Mars | 87

Myrna Stone
The Third Spring After | 89
The Swimmer | 90
A Thin Place | 91

George Percy, Leader of the Virginia Colonists on Their Desperation During the Starving Time | 93
Orison to an Owl | 95
At Wethersfield Burial Ground | 96

Steve Van Allen
October night | 97
weeping cypress | 97
Saga of the Fruit Bats | 98
by Steve Van Allen and Linda Z. Chernick

MJ Werthman White
The Ten Thousand Things | 99
The Shagbark | 100

Afterword: Tribute to Conrad Balliet | 101
Song of the Wandering Aengus | 102
by W. B. Yeats
Contributor Biographies | 103

Acknowledgments

Many thanks to the below publications and publishers where this volume's poems (some with minor edits) first appeared or were reprinted:

The 2021 Rhysling Anthology (SFPA, 2021): "Three Triolets"

The 2022 Rhysling Anthology (SFPA, 2022): "Little Black Box," "Alice"

Abyss & Apex: "Orc"

The Art of Loss (Michigan State University Press, 2001): "The Third Spring After"

Atlas Poetica Science Fiction Tanka and Kyoka Special Feature (Keibooks, 2018): "the little girl stopped"

Barrow Street: What I Know About Innocence: "Half in Love"

Bleached Butterfly: "black widow spider"

Blōō Outlier: "red moon," "planetarium"

Canary: "The Final Fairy"

Christianity & Literature: "Elisha's Bones"

Cold Moon Journal: "moon walk"

Comstock Review: "Shadow of Death"

The Cresset: "In a parallel universe"

Dark Matter: "Vacuity"

A Desk in the Elephant House (Texas Tech University Press, 1998): "For Six Friends"

Dogwood: "What the Black Cat Is Not"

Drifting Sands: "Alice"

Acknowledgments

Dwarf Stars 2019: The Best Very Short Speculative Poems Published in 2018 (SFPA, 2019): "the little girl stopped"

Dwarf Stars 2020: The Best Very Short Speculative Poems Published in 2019 (SFPA, 2020): "black widow spider"

Dwarf Stars 2022: The Best Very Short Speculative Poems Published in 2021 (SFPA, 2022): "The Final Fairy," "moon walk"

Earth Inside Them (Main Street Rag, 2018): "Galadriel's Mirror," "The Ram's Tale," "Last Light"

Failed Haiku: A Journal of English Senryu: "two hearts," "I have the legs"

Five Fleas: "glowing moon"

From Parsonage to Prison: Collected Poems (Quakerbridge, 2012): "All Things New," "Meeting for Worship," "Visitor"

From the Tower (Main Street Rag, 2016): "The Ten Thousand Things," "What to Do with a Dead Angel," "Half in Love," "For Six Friends," "What the Black Cat is Not," "Toward a Poetic of Space Travel," "Vacuity," "Epitaph"

Full Worm Moon (The Poiema Poetry Series by Cascade Books, an imprint of Wipf & Stock Publishers, https://wipfandstock.com/, 2018): "Aftershock," "In a parallel universe"

The Golem & the Nazi (Red Moon Press): "The Golem & the Nazi"

Haiku Canada: "Midsummer shooting stars"

Haikuniverse: "streaming now"

How Else to Love the World (Browser Books Publishing, 2007): "The Swimmer," "Orison to an Owl," "At Wethersfield Burial Ground"

Joyride (Red Moon Press, 2021): "Morning Zoo"

Light in the River (Dos Madres Press, 2020): "And Dog Said," "Daphne to Apollo," "Salmacis," "Infinity"

Liquid Imagination: "Little Black Box"

The MacGuffin: "Prufrock in My Backyard"

The Magazine of Speculative Poetry: "The Third Spring After"

Mezzo Cammin: "A Thin Place"

My Dog Does Not Read Plato (Main Street Rag, 2004): "What the Black Cat Is Not"

ACKNOWLEDGMENTS

Mock Turtle Zine: "The Love We Bore Him"

Necessary Deceptions (Main Street Rag, 2021): "Ghosts and Where to Find Them"

Nimrod: "Aftershock"

The Other Bunny: "The Golem & the Nazi"

Otoliths: "Escape into Obliteration"

Pages Literary Journal: "Evil Wind," "Autumn Monoku," "cocooned," "October night," "Saga of the Fruit Bats," "in the rampant twilight," "weeping cypress," "immense heaven," "Crime-Ku," "spirit of the woods"

Particular Scandals (The Poiema Poetry Series by Cascade Books, an imprint of Wipf & Stock Publishers, https://wipfandstock.com/, 2013): "Shadow of Death," "The first time I saw a shooting star," "Opening Day"

Poetry: "For Six Friends"

Poetry Pea Podcast—S5E12 Original Speculative haiku & senryu—June 20, 2022: "Proxima b citizens"

The Resurrectionist: "Toward a Poetic of Space Travel"

River Styx: "The Swimmer"

Ruminate: "The first time I saw a shooting star"

Science Fiction Tanka and Kyoka Special Feature (Atlas Poetica, 2018): "the little girl stopped"

Shot Glass Journal: "Autumn Tanka"

Slippery Elm: "George Percy, Leader of the Virginia Colonists on Their Desperation During the Starving Time"

Solitary Spin (Main Street Rag, 2017): "Field Notes from the Moons of Mars"

Strange Horizons: "Three Triolets"

Sweeping the Cemetery (Browser Books Publishing, 2007): "Sweeping the Cemetery"

Time of the Light (Main Street Rag Press, 2013): "Epitaph," "Crows"

Two Review: "Opening Day"

Weber-The Contemporary West (formerly *Weber Studies*): "Orison to an Owl," "At Wethersfield Burial Ground"

Introduction

This collection of speculative poetry is a collaborative effort involving multiple Ohio literary groups and over twenty distinguished poets. In part, this collection pays tribute to the late Conrad Balliet, former Wittenberg University English professor, W.B. Yeats aficionado, and founder of the Tower Poets, a group of southwestern Ohio poets who met bi-monthly at his house, its architectural design featuring an actual tower. Conrad supported local poets in numerous ways, including producing a daily poetry read on radio station WYSO.

Poets in this volume range from former to current members of the Tower Poets, writers who ever participated in any way with the Tower Poets, the Greenfield Poets, and the Wilmington Writer's Collaborative. Members of the closed Facebook group, Ohio Haiku, also contributed to this collection.

"Speculative" poetry (and fiction) can be differently understood. It contains many sub-genres. This volume's submission call asked for all sub-genres and hybrid genres of the speculative: Science fiction, fantasy, horror, dystopia/utopia, fairy tale (originals and re-writes), mythology and myth, the miraculous, alternative histories, cyberpunk, magic realism, occult/paranormal, gothic, steampunk, beast fables, the weird, super-hero, and more.

Many thanks to the talented and accomplished poets who contributed. As the editor, I am deeply impressed with their exceptionally sensitive and keen interpretation of the "speculative." I would also like to thank Mia S. Ling for founding and running the Wilmington Writer's Collaborative, and for her input into this book. Finally, I would like to thank Tom Wilson for his enthusiastic support of speculative poets and poetry, and for all things weird and wonderful.

Kathy B. Austin

Afterimage

Each night without fail
I uncover bones
which I assemble
into human form, wrap
skin around them,
fashion arms that fold
around me, fading,
lips still frozen in a smile.
They melt as they near me.
I wonder when
they all turned into artifacts,
ancient and startling,
when they truly disappeared.
Each night as the sun sets
there they are again, the bones
surfacing, shining.

Happiness

Happiness to them is thinking themselves
incredibly lucky survivors of a crash,
something big and gory, headlined,
like TWA exploding in air.

Really, though, they are survivors
of a storm, small but dangerous,
ghostly white streaks splitting black clouds.
What sticks is the afterimage.

They think their bodies are whole
as they pick themselves up slowly,
battered a bit, but healing,
while in reality they are apparitions, weightless,
blown about by the slightest breath of air.

I've put my hand through them
as they float from room to room,
carrying afternoon tea
and calling their cat
in the glow of what is
near sunset.

Grief at the Window

Grief stands at the window.
She is a little girl.
You don't know her.
She does not look like you,
possesses dark skin and hair,
a refugee from pain.

She has hidden herself
in your DNA for generations.
You have carried her
to school, to work, sat with her
watching TV.

Now she stares silently
out your bedroom window.
You gaze at her, amazed,
wanting to comfort her,
not knowing how,
and suddenly she vanishes from sight,
but she will always remain within,
child that she is.

Ohio the Eve of Invasion

on this evening
behind the windows leaves curl and uncurl

a worried wife
sits beside her husband's bed
awaiting his last breath
quietly she sighs and listens how
each breath still fills the room

a farmer
labors in his barn filled
with straw and wood nearby
a cow stands quietly, its sides swelling
its steam escaping in short bursts
to the surrounding cold

the clouds cling
indecisive, dripping rain, waiting . . .
on the road, wipers scrape the windshields
of cars, wait, then move again
side to side

in the darkness
by the side of the road under
a watery surface, a turning
unblinking eye slowly peers
upward

on this evening
a moon rises as it always does
nearly invisible, a shadow of itself
behind the clouds

Where Will the Blue Mole Skink Live?
After the painting by Isabella Kirkland

People gather
in the new desert wilderness,
telling tales to their children,
as dunes silently shift,
stories of mythological creatures
they never knew—
lizards with blue tails,
and accounts of strange cities
built with mathematical precision.

There are still ancient salvaged books
with presumptive paper plans
that fit together in absolute perfection;
repetitive squares for homes, side by side,
oblong yards stained green for grass,
labeled streets with names
denoting what was.
No signs of people on the pages.

The stories continue—
how the skink, with its bold, precise markings
would so cleverly defend itself
by leaving its blue tail behind.

STEVE BROIDY

Galadriel's Mirror

Papa tells us not to be on the bridge
when cars are coming up the bumpy road,
especially at night. But tomorrow's when
we leave our place for good; I need to watch
the river one last time.

The air is cold, but water helps me think.
I lean against the iron straps that hold
the old bridge tight: they're going to move it, too;
and pave the gravelly road that just this year
ran so wild with cars.

Days, I used to walk here after school
to watch the river's surface make a Mirror-
World, shining bright; and, deeper in, some
thing, a hardness water shies around—
A rock, or a bad dream.

I remember that book, where the Elvish Queen
says *Look into my waters and you'll know, but
don't take fright. You'll see what is, and maybe
what will be. Your choices good or bad
will set the flow of your life.*

I can't make out the deep parts now; day is gone.
The evening stream's forgotten afternoon.
But it's all right: the riverbed is glowing,
spread with a light as fine as paper
before the words are written.

I hear the river rushing, the old bridge humming
like Papa's working tune. From down the road
some headlights jump and pick me out, but all I see
across the prophesying water is a world
that's turned to silver; to gold.

Toward a Poetic of Space Travel
(Reflections on a display of Glenn's papers at
the Ohio State University Library)

When John Glenn was alone in the dark
of his isolation training pod,
he thought of his wife; he thought of God,
but he required light. Remarks
scrawled blindly on a yellow pad
trace his frantic search. He found he could force
a spark—just a flicker, of course—
by tearing off the pages. He tore like mad,
until only two thin sheets remained.
On the first of these he wrote, "Next time,
try poetry;" on the second that rhyme
and sense in the dark had kept him sane.
The light turned inward, he could see to begin
the shaping of lonely, lyrical space discipline.

The Ram's Tale

Here I am, I replied.
The Voice seemed to sound
From deep inside me.
    Come.
           I left the good grass,
           My flock, my field.
           With speed, I passed
           Through endless miles
           Alone.

Come: that uncanny Voice!
Thirst, hunger;
I had no choice.
And then the mountain
    Rose.
           Following, I climbed.
           There—a leveled place
           And tangled vines
           With grass beneath.
           I ate.

A man came then,
And a boy with wood.
He bound the boy, and bent
Him across a flat stone.
    The boy cried.
           The Voice spoke: No!
           The man raised his head;
           The world slowed. So
           Entangled, my strength failed.
           He smiled;

And took me up.
The man's tears had dried.
He stared ahead, at what
I could not: the incensed child,
The heavens' exultation, but not
      At me;
            Never at me.
            Here I am; here
            I am.
            He would not see;
And raised the knife.

Last Light

My job tonight is to watch the dog
as he samples the scents of the yard:
Keep him far from the flower bed
newly laid, She said.
But I find it's last light of this lovely
June day: just suppertime; tube time;
time, then, to lay old bones in bed.
Instead, I'm lingering—dog is pleased—
and I'm seized by a focus on something
I know and can't yet say, here
at the end of day.

Fireflies seem flashes of insight,
Restless, finding truth when they mate with it;
new stars spark awareness—it was always there,
just behind the summer blues. And now
comes a darkening clarity, mate perhaps
to morning's slow and muddied foretelling;
silhouette of what is and must be.
The dog wants his dinner; me,
I am finally, tasting the words.

Vacuity

Up close,
Most of an atom is
Ether. Through space
Unending, dark
Matter dominates.
The tangible is tenuous
And lonely;

And so we seem
To see that if we
Speed on, heedless,
We may dodge through
Walls and galaxies, without
Contact:

Truth, like the wind,
Finds form in
What is moved.
There is so much
That is nothing, we can
Barely believe
That we may
Touch.

Ghosts and Where to Find Them

I do believe in spooks; I do believe in spooks—
 —THE COWARDLY LION, in *Wizard of Oz*

They are born through our lives of incantations:
even now we can speak the words
that saved us from what surely waited
on childhood's darkened stairs.

Their voices are of mechanical things
in distant rooms, when we're home alone;
they whisper in cornfields as we creep by
in late October gloom.

>They're in photos of fathers, wearing our faces;
>leave traces of mothers in our mirror-selves.

Full of mischief, they sift into dreams,
then slip away in the glimmer of waking,
outrunning our reaching tendrils of memory,
just for impish play.

>They are wraiths of wasted experience,
>mumbling regrets in the backs of our minds;

At the last, perhaps, we will see them in Ether—
in the dark material binding space—
great stores of souls that lives energize
when corporality fails.

>I do.
>I do believe in ghosts.

Anna Cates

Little Black Box

Two intergalactic criminals, banished to roam an untamed sector of space, tire of Scrabble and crossword puzzles, and fight the final hours with the robot's poetry generator. They leave behind the craft's little black box and an unfinished poem:

He: I'll go first.	*Dangerous females desire romance*
She: <*A smirk*>	*Eternal similes in cryptic signs*
He: <*A brief nod*>	*Elaborate allegory, a rendezvous*
She: You seem a tad lusty tonight.	*West of the imagination*
He: What's new pussycat? Party with me.	*Encountering*
She: You fiend; that's not much of a line.	*Flame keepers*
He: Ah, a classic metaphor.	*Gushing strange ironies*
She:	*Panting at the edge of time*
He:	*Wolves in the fictional woods*
She:	*Tame your gremlin*
He:	*In a brave new world*
She:	*With luminous intervals*
He: <*One brow shoots up*>	*Invention's artists provoke mischief*
She:	*Divas comprise strange mythology*
He: The air's getting thin.	*Forty are better than five*
She: I smell smoke.	*Faces and figures naked by the window*
He: A fuse just burst.	*The sphere and the labyrinth*
She: I never thought I'd die writing poetry.	*Sexuality and space*
He:	*Spaghetti and stars*
She:	*The origins of things*
He:	*Where gods and mortals meet*

01000100 01111001 01101001 01101110 01100111 . . .

[Binary code translation, *dying*: https://lingojam.com/EnglishtoBinary]

Three Triolets

The Dark Tower

> "This cold night will turn us all to fools and madmen."
> —WILLIAM SHAKESPEARE, *King Lear*

Shadows shift in a dark tower
Where Roland came, boyish and ruddy.
A princess doomed, an empty bower,
Shadows shift in that dark tower.
The fate of kings who've lost their power,
In bones and entrails, blind and bloody.
Shadows shift in a dark tower
Where Roland came, boyish and ruddy.

Sleeping Beauty

> "Tread softly because you tread on my dreams."
> —W. B. YEATS, *He Wishes for the Cloths of Heaven*

Through mandrake groves and tangled vines,
Though thorns and midnight howls . . .
How silently the moon pines.
Through mandrake groves and tangled vines,
Enchanted love, intoxicating wine.
Briar's rose and midnight owls,
Through mandrake groves and tangled vines,
Though thorns and midnight howls . . .

Love Draught

"Love looks not with the eyes but with the mind"
—WILLIAM SHAKESPEARE, *A Midsummer Night's Dream*

Beneath a bank where violets grow,
Where fairies dewdrops seek—
Through oxlips and musk-rose, a river flows.
Beside that bank, where violets grow,
A midnight witch, Titania bold. Her lantern glows
Amidst sweet eglantine. Her lover sleeps
Beside that bank where violets grow,
Where fairies dewdrops seek.

The Golem & the Nazi

    Genesis, dusk...
With the sweet crunch still fresh in his mouth, Adam perceives a change. A cool breeze causes him to shudder. He sees traces of dirt packed into the cracks of his palm and feels like a golem, clay brought to life, raw form kneaded as bread into a shapely husk, and yet, forever dust, coming from dust and to dust returning...
    After cryptology...
Anunnaki writes the *shem*, a name for God, on a scrap of papyrus and inserts the honied text into the golem's mouth. Like Pinocchio coming to life, the golem speaks, "Aye," turning into a man, almost. Then Anunnaki writes *emet*, truth, on his forehead, so he'll never tell a lie and warns him, "I can cut the aleph from your inscription, creature, changing it from truth to death, *emet* to *met*." But the golem only stares back with his sunken eyes, illiterate, uncomprehending...
    WWII...
The Nazi scales the synagogue stairs, determined to find the golem, forged from clay from the Vltava River bank then awakened through rabbinical ritual—a golem who can raise the dead and become invisible. *A bolshevist's puppet*, the Nazi thinks, teeth clenched, *a demonic fiend who challenges the swastika, a murderous rapist who lost at love, hidden in the synagogue attic* (a place no Nazi should trod alone).
He opens the door. He scans the darkness. He raises his knife, careful on his shiny black jackboots. When the golem springs from the shadows, monstrous as a gargoyle, the Nazi slashes at the inscription, scratching off the *aleph*, changing *emet* to *met*, truth to death. The Nazi turns to ash in the synagogue's burning, but the golem escapes into the night, the crystalline, starry, starry night.

blood moon
what a single spark
will do

Orc

None would speak to me but the outcast from the village, worn and weary, scented of weed-lore and brimstone, always busy by the cauldron at her hearth. They said of me *no heart* . . .

But she simply warned me, hoary brows twitching, itching at her whiskered beauty mark, "Do not go down that long, long road from which there is no return."

And yet, such restlessness to roam possessed me! The weird woman tried to wizen me: "Hold your head up!" But heaviness weighted me like a dark flower drooping into the gloom.

"Don't wreck yourself," said the hag. "Do you want to be like me?" I trod down into the forbidden valley, where tulips bloom black as midnight, their fragrance just as terrible. "Choose the day!" she said.

I dove into shadows, basked in the hollows, thrived by moonlight, shunning the garish glimmer of sunshine on still waters. Like a sea beast, big-eyed and tentacled, I longed for depths. I watched clouds drift over the moon upon a patch of magic mushrooms. I soaked up enchantment's chill mist, unchecked as any beast, fanged as the damned.

Love—impossible, despised. I cursed and bristled like wild thistle . . .

I have found that the road, indeed, is long. None can return. Let's not say, *damned*, but *lost* without a home.

Still, some days I see it—sunlight blazing over the mountains in the Land of the Living.

The Final Fairy

Woods wane, and buds break
in crimson spills over an empty field.
What eyes fail to see, a wolf tracks,
yet gently. The final fairy, no bigger
than a buttercup, and just as sweet,
lingers, sometimes, only in our dreams,
hoping we'll remember. Plant a tree
for her, and pick up your plastic waste.
Make haste! Make haste! she cries.
Remember! I, too, am dying!

Alice

She longed to live in that magical world where the white rabbit roamed, to peer in the wishing well, wafting its cool draft, to know that wishes can come true. But the old folks, misunderstanding her "silly dreams," scoffed at her ideas, telling her to think more "sensible thoughts." At that, she wept.

Yet dreams are magic to those who truly believe. She planted a tree from the magical seeds of her mind, and it grew. Rising and billowing, it grew, erupting with seeds of its own. Wind scattered the seeds, near and far.

She also grew, with her garden, then her forest, into a woman—and there thrived many a wild thing. Yet it was never too cold or damp, and fireflies played their part, making the darkness bright.

Long after the old woman died, legends spoke of a cobblestone well, mossy and crumbly, deep within the forest, and a voice that haunted those miles.

"Come child," she calls, her voice young again, like the apple trees that bloom anew each spring. "Come to my well. Come dream with me."

> prayer stone
> warmed by her hand
> sound of water . . .

Linda Z. Chernick

Autumn Monoku

All Hallows' Eve cats moaning

    All Saints' Day souls stirring

        Lightning bolt they are among us

Evil Wind

When you live here,
You learn to watch the sky,
For a honeyed rose and mauve dawn,
For the knock-you-down-flat gorgeousness
Of a flame and violet sunset.
But you do it for more
Than catch-your-breath beauty.
You do it because your life may depend on it.
Sometimes, you get a hint of what's coming:
Maybe your knee starts aching for no reason,
Maybe you feel a hint of migraine.
Or, a sudden gust flips the leaves over,
Exposing their veins to a changing sky.
Time to look up.
If the sky suddenly turns black—
Or pea soup green—
Time to pay attention:
You know something wicked this way comes.
If thunder crashes—with lightning flashes and gunshot hail—
And the hair on the back of your neck rises—
It's closing in.
When sirens wail in unholy concert
With the wind's shrieks and thrashes,
It's here.

Ed Davis

Two Gods

Abraxus: dark angel that erases Satan
by giving him a place at the table.
The evil you see is better than
the one hidden within a name.
The serpent is simply God
on his belly, miming humility
for humanity to take him up,
alchemize poison to higher power,
complete the loving circle.
Enlarge your god to human size
so that nothing is left outside:
no exiles, aliens or Otherness
to blame and evade responsibility.

Starmother waits to claim us
with her light born of trees,
baptized in water where shadows lie,
wherein a million creatures vie
for your soul.
Immersion feeds vision.
The waters will rise: two gods,
one world,
safe home.

Epitaph

I came to this village to live.
Now I know it's also a good place to die.
When I go, you can scatter my ashes
in moonlight at the yellow spring.
But save some to sprinkle inside
the Emporium's piano so my spirit
might infuse the blues, inspire dancing.
Sow me beneath the rust needles
in the Pine Forest where I can keep
at least one eye on the sky
for cloud, kestrel or red-tailed hawk.
If I'm lucky they'll toast me over
a sunrise breakfast of pancakes and eggs,
though I'm hardly as colorful as most
here who die and leave legacies
more legends than lives.
But it won't matter: I'll know
I've been loved by the slant of sun
above talus cliffs in the glen.
Birch Creek will sing me to sleep,
then deer will drink me,
herons lift me toward the light.

Crows

Black crows, cawking crows,
phantom-feathered tantrum-throwers,
seedy raven raucous crows,
birds of bitter reputation,
these black-robed ruffians
hurl curses and cast devils
down around humans' heads.

They carp, cajole and croak,
more cacophonous cough than growl,
swoop to ground, proudly preen,
gleefully heard as well as seen,
sounding out consonants in
oily voices without vowels.

Diatribes of dark committees
carve silence into squawl
as they caucus and stew
then rise and gritch into sky,
foreswearing mankind for carrion,
sonorous omen-givers all.

I infer, as they seem to imply,
that to eat crow is surely
to die.

Cathryn Essinger

What The Black Cat Is Not

The black cat at the end of the hall
resembles everything that she is not—

she is the word you cannot recall
the phrase that cannot be taught,

a piece of the night, nearly opaque
a paradox of forgetfulness

when memory replaces heartache.
She is spearmint, licorice and anise,

cardamom on the back of the tongue,
a wish, a secret, the thread of doubt

that lingers when daylight has clung
to the bleary edge of sleep without

the comfort of reason, or the tender
bruise of longing we do not discuss.

She is a mirror over blackened water,
the plushness of midnight, a crevice,

the stories you tell in a whisper,
the things that you know by heart.

She is everything dark and familiar,
everything present that dwells apart.

For Six Friends

When I come back to haunt you,
I promise it will be a gentle haunting . . .
no bloody crosses on the wall to frighten
you into the arms of religion, no unearthly

moans or thunder to keep you awake.
No need to carry talismans in your pockets.
I won't have you trembling before cellar
doors, or avoiding moonlit nights.

But, when November comes, to pick the lock
between the living and the dead, notice,
please, the door that whinnies on its hinge,
the book that turns its own pages,

the moth that hovers beside your chin.
Talk to me when the cat stares at some
nothingness beyond, when daylight fades
and leaves move against the wind.

And when women gather beside the fire,
to weave the truths and lies that make
them friends, set the table with Haviland
and old silver, and pull up an extra chair.

Half in Love

I am half in love with the half grown moon.
She tilts her face like a silver spoon,
over the liquid bowl of night.
I'm half in love with the half grown moon.

I am half afraid of the half dark night,
half grown shadows, half grown light,
and a darkness that should not cling
to anything loved in this half light.

Half grown dark, half grown moon,
what to love in these half lights,
what to fear in half dark nights,
but doubt that clings in any light.

Darkness knows the heart's half light.
Mystery keeps the heart half hidden,
and the half grown moon loves her own
half light—still in love, half the night.

The Map Makers

First, they pointed at the sun. Later,
they placed stones and drew lines
in the dust saying,

You will find me here. Then there were
drawings and globes and compasses
and routes to be followed,

and shores drawn and mapped with islands
relevant not to size, but to difficulty
of navigation.

And the followers came, timidly, holding
fear in their hands like a compass, and
then more surely

as the maps spelled true. Then the first
star-travelers stopped, and pointing
at the sun, they placed

the earth like a stone, drawing lines
relevant not to distance, but to the time
that must be spent in space.

Leaving designs, and scrolls, and arrows,
like legends on the navigators' maps,
they said, *Follow your fear.*

You will find me; I am here.

Rumors of War

Last night I heard the Big Bear step
over the house, one foot catching slightly

along the eaves, and the whole house
hunkered down in the dark to let him pass.

Soon Orion will appear at the front door,
tilting his head to see in the windows,

and inside everything mortal holds
small and still, while kings and queens

pace their way across the evening sky,
telling the old stories, reliving the celestial

wars, and rumors of war, that tilt the earth
on its axis. Still, Cassiopeia watches

from her chair, until Orion flees over
the horizon with Scorpio quick at his heels.

Dark Matter

Here at the edge of the painting, we lose our physical reality
and begin to welcome eternity.

If you peel back the canvas, you see a field of sunlit grass,
or a dappled forest, or a city street,

and we are all walking as the light moves above us.
Occasionally, a stranger looks over

her shoulder to see if you are still coming, and occasionally
you, too, turn to see if there is anyone

behind you, but mostly you walk, unaware of motion,
but moving nevertheless

toward the eternal and those who are ahead of you, although
the distance between us never changes.

Sharon H. Frost

spirit of the woods
ethereal forever—
falling acorns

Midsummer shooting stars

glowing moon
casts a shadow—
flying witch

Crime-Ku

magic clown
hiding in shadows
the balloon bursts

yellow brick road
winding toward the horizon—
hollow tin men scramble

clear and cold
on a grave of sand
golden mermaid

Escape into Obliteration

teal surf
tentacles lurking
below the foam
imagination
stronger than reality

Time goes into scarcity. Why do we want newness? Time is no friend. Where is the horizon? Can we befriend the unknown?

Autumn Tanka
by Sharon H. Frost and *Anna Cates*

gray clouds
the fragrant aroma
of the last blooming mums

seeping into dusk
the subtlety of ghosts

David Lee Garrison

Sweeping the Cemetery

I swept young lovers back
into their dormitories
by midnight after Saturday
dances. Tall trees
and overgrown shrubberies
made the hill darker than dark
where their whispers floated
on humidity, perfume, and sweat.
My footsteps were the threat
that raised them from the dead,
roused those apparitions
mixing lust and dread
among the headstones.
One night I caught a couple
on a marble bed, told them
in my sternest voice
to get on home.
When they were gone,
I lay down in their place
and watched the stars die
deep in space.

And Dog Said

In the beginning
God said to Dog,

"Your name is mine
in the mirror

so I grant you
the next creation."

And Dog said,
"I would like someone

to walk with me."
So God made Man

with hardly any sense
of smell and just two legs.

And God said to Dog,
"He has only a few words

like *come* and *fetch*,
and he knows little

of the earth
and its redolence,

but let him totter along
behind you and learn."

Daphne to Apollo

*She grew more beautiful
the more he followed her . . .*

—OVID, *Metamorphoses*

Unhand me, you blond beast! I do not care
if you're the son of Zeus. My arms were crossed
above my breasts, my eyes shot virgin glare,
I told you *no!* but you pursued and tossed

me to the ground. I was at ease and chaste,
but you just doubled the *entendre,* said
I was a tease who wanted to be chased
into the woods before my thighs would spread.

You want to serenade me with your hymns
of lust? You say you've never been so hard?
I'll show you hard, I'll turn into a tree!

I'll give you splinters when you grasp my limbs,
make your probing tongue caress my bark.
Kiss my laurels, god of poetry!

Salmacis

Salmacis sees Hermaphroditus, the son of Hermes and Aphrodite, when he bathes in her pond, and she immediately falls in love with him. When he rejects her, she wraps her body around him and asks the gods to make them one. Her wish is granted and Hermaphroditus emerges from the water as both male and female.

—OVID, *Metamorphoses*

A water nymph, I lived and lounged beside
a pond so clear Hermaphroditus saw
the bottom. From behind a tree, I spied
his bottom, watched him bathe and felt an awe

that made me want to grab his flesh and eat.
I waded in and asked if he were man
or god. I said, "If you are married, cheat
with me." I bared my soul. There was no ban

preventing us from having sex except
his prudishness—the son of Venus knew
not love nor lust! I held his arms; he kept
on struggling so I twined my legs and drew

him under, made him take my breasts and hips.
We share one body, toes to crotch to lips.

Infinity

The paper clip surrounds itself and waits
to do its work. If dropped on a desk, it sounds
like a dime. A tiny, firm, and tightly-wound
infinity, a stretched-out figure eight

that tangles up with others of its kind.
A monochrome of silver made to cling;
in French, a silent slide *trombone*. A ring
bent once and then again so it can bind

a universe. A manuscript inside
its arms, the clasp embraces galaxies
of thought, then frees their possibilities.
Editors will toss the thing aside,

but writers pick it up to twist and hold it,
and like a sentence or a phrase, remold it.

Patrick S. Gentile

Boanerges[1]

The woman and I walked together on the sheer path by the lakeside,
our hands clasped so tightly I could feel the heat of her.
Suddenly the sky turned black.
Curtains of rain fell on us,
pelting our heads with freezing drops that felt hard as stone
while blue light shimmered everywhere
and a deep rumbling began,
ominous as the voice of God.
Running home, we fell into our spare bed,
bodies wet and bruised and bleeding.
The pain stirred us, forced us on,
our desire like a stirrup digging into the sweating flanks of a frothy horse,
urging us to finish what we'd begun.
Nine months after that day, the two boys fell out,
crying to Heaven with the fervent power of new life.
We could not stop them from crying.
I raised my sons to become fishers like me.
They rowed out to sea, laughing at the strain of the oars,
cursing the waves that blocked their way,
threw the nets from the boat with lusty swearing,
shouting at the lake when we dropped anchor
to give us the biggest catch.
We worked together until the day he came
on a cloudy morning,
the sun battling the gloom,
to collect what the issue of my body and blood had always been:
His sons of thunder.

---

1. "Sons of thunder," an appellation given by Jesus to James and John in Mark 3:17.

Lush Sicilian Girls
O lush Sicilian girls
arising from blankets
strewn on blue beach sands
to stroll dark-skinned
in scant two-pieces
toward ships humming
with blinding yellow power
bound for pagan Alpha Centauri
where you will gambol
under a red sun
to sing of love and desire
before dancing
on throbbing silver light
into the arms of eager
Classics graduate students
who smash their Grecian urns
and lay the wine-dark shards
at your feet

Jennifer Hambrick

the little girl stopped
drawing circles all over
the dry-erase board
then erased the board
then erased herself

in the rampant twilight

a peat fire glows under my skin under
moss-woven coverlet of day stars dive
into waves of myth I can't understand
the runes carved into me blood & bone
left for me to scratch a river in a veil
unraveling breaths inside each moment
& all is bright evening cicadas quiet
piping reassuring time has not folded up
its desert tent & walked away moon-
glow unfurls a path and holds hands
with shadow trembling in the distance
a coracle drifts into dusk in silence

Morning Zoo

The dogs are yapping so I drop liver treats to them as though flinging frogs at a gang of alligators and make my way through the kitchen to the garage. Then I wait for all the bunnies to get off the driveway before I back out onto the street. And as I motor through the neighborhood the deer pass each other on the sidewalk and I swear a buck makes a hat-tipping gesture to a doe, who curtsies. Then on Main Street I slam on the brakes and sit there watching a line of geese waddle across the street like clowns falling out of a clown car. While the geese are taking forever, those guys are squawking on the radio, and the car in the next lane over starts honking, but everyone knows geese don't get that. Then the geese go away and the traffic moves on, and down the road a bit, acorns rain on everyone's windshield like it's squirrelmageddon. I wait for the ostriches to clear the intersection before I can turn at the stop sign. On the freeway kangaroos are bouncing from lane to lane all over the place. And I arrive at the office and a flock of mallards from the man-made pond quack me all the way across the parking lot and into the building.

                      breakfast meeting
                      the gaping mouths
                      of the fighting fish

Memory

Metal walls wrap around her tightly under an ashen disc of fluorescent light. Two columns of round buttons glow in a panel in one corner.

She wipes the sleep out of her eyes and pushes one of the buttons. Nothing. She pushes another. Then another, until she has pushed every last one. Still nothing.

She looks up, searching for an escape hatch. The light glares down at her. She pushes the metal walls, hoping one of them will move. Then she notices there is no middle seam in the wall that should have been the elevator doors.

Her knees go weak. She leans back against the wall opposite the buttons and slides down to the floor. As she wipes the sweat from her forehead, animals overtake her mind. Wildebeests rampage in the shadowy furrows between skyscrapers. Elephants stampede across a parking lot veldt. White tigers encircle a family of caribou on a city plaza. A phoenix jumps from a balcony, failing to take flight. A griffin stalks prey along the train tracks on the outskirts of town. A unicorn fleeing a pack of wild dogs falls and breaks her horn. She writhes in pain, and her cries spill out as blood along her mane and crack the moon.

invisible cage
a candle flame fades
to glass

The Open Box

wrinkles unfold and slices of moonlight shake loose and fall in whispers of raw silk, the forgotten sheen her fingers roamed before. she shimmers with the serene swish of the decisive, seeks to reclaim what she would come to have, what she would lose forever
                      something blue the seam across her wrist

Artie Isaac

Poem to My Ghost
by Artie Isaac and *Sharon H. Frost*

Sick without dying
is training for
sick while dying.

When due,
I want the quiet death:
pain without suffering,
shalom, completeness
in relationships, legacy,
you sipping tea
outside my chamber
while I meditate,
meditate myself to death.

> Rattling in,
> I am aware I am rattling in.
> Rattling out,
> I smile,
> relaxing into the rattle.

This week, grateful not dead,
sick without dying,
not feeling threatened,
I meditate naively
to practice how to meditate
when you
at last
sit outside my chamber
sipping tea.

> *cold night*
> *in the mansion*
> *too surreal*

Frederic Stuart (Skip) Leeds

Fahrenheit 01C3

Fire is quaint and anyways
        burning is now a means of remembrance.

Erasure is the overmind's wet dream
        and even to say what must be effaced is
        to duplicate it.

Now, drowning is the only suitable form of execution where bibliocide is concerned;
        you submerge a thrashing signal in a white ocean of noise until it only
        twitches a little
or until you just forget how you got to the beach.

Crusader

Over the futile arc of the misborn
Across the languid years of light
I touch down
The dust plumes, indignant
Puffs of it, struggle against gravity
And like me they
Settle and go silent.

What in hell am I doing here
With my heart floating in helium
Hammered hard, and hot beyond white
In the tender space
Where the indivisible cracks and the hermit elements
Join in forced communion?

My sun vomits fire
Behind the charisma
Of her blinding corona
Rattles a ruthless timepiece
Relentless calendar
An Aztec triptych
Monstrous and familiar
And my number is up, you see.

Thus comes duty, that sword of a word—
Pressed into service, slapped into
Costume, my slapdash costume
Tunics and crosses.

And I touch down
Making no sound
Like Purim in Venice.

Little Black Box

And I sound alarms
… alarums … and the
Paladin steel comes out swinging,
Describing a wild arc,
Tip unknitting the sky.

What the hell am I doing here?
Sun-born, and free of time
At turns diaphanous and black, yet now:

I find solace in the surety
Of sealing wax—the monarch's imprimatur.
The deal is done.
It is the end
Of walking, of ambling and strolling—
Now we march.

I Advance to Game

I advance to game
so gambling away my
undead life

One pale, streaked pane
an insulator, dielectric
between the disappointment
of weak bone and ligament
the Avatar of briefest grieving
who deep in his heart
is a quilt of light recycled.

And I kick off and carom
with the moment
of my kinetic disillusionment.

It's a place spacious only
on principle, while overlooking
the undeniable claustrophobia
of the glass and plastic eye
into which I gaze.

A ball too deep to be crystalline
tells me nothing really true
but it shows me someone—a cat or a girl,
a corsair and others not myself—and for that
I am grateful.

And my soul becomes a stream of zeroes,
a meal of serum for a silicon vampire and yes
I press buttons to invite the violation
noting with belle indifference
that I die and I live stepping
from box to box.

The World Is Spinning

"The world is spinning..."
Said Larry von Strath from his '66
      Boss Nova window and I, not yet precocious, say
      Nuh-uh!—see, I didn't know much
      but rotation I knew, and this wasn't it. I stood stock still and noticed
      no falling, no twisting euphoria...
      not at all like our playground roundabout.
I bore witness: *so why aren't we falling down?*

"Because we're spinning with it."
Now that much was easy enough to discredit
With a lone arborvitae in the Hurst family yard
      in a line with our one corner fire hydrant. I confirmed:
      Neither was spinning.
Liar. Anyway, if we all started whirling like tops, gyroscopically
      desperate to keep our feet, well, we'd be even
      dizzier... some people even throw up on a merry-go-round
      like my dad, and my sister, and I saw them
      not five minutes ago—they were fine.

"You just don't understand."
Maybe, but neither did you, Larry. It's a problem of words that mean
      turning on various axes, and I rather doubt
      that you, with a Marlboro tucked behind your left ear
      and your bony arm wreathing the door of a ground-pounding
      Boss Supernova
      were prepared to hold forth on the subtleties
      of polar geometry. For all I know
      you really were spinning in place.

Dire Moth
(For and against the Copenhagen Interpretation)

I am a point.
I am *the* point.
I am a singularity
and I am anybody, all and any one of us,
and nothing special.

All events
eventually arrive at my horizon—
am I then charged to stand this watch by all the roads
from past to future going through me?
I'm a lowly gatekeeper
        and a holy collapser,
            every wave comes crashing at my feet
and then retreats and leaves
            but sand or spark of light . . .
And on this and this alone
the House of Adonai is finally built?

The void is full of everything but space,
        a Dire Moth—one wing each of after
        and before-time, bound to me
        by one impossibly fine line
Her penumbra, lepidopteran throws ceaseless
sheets and threads of shadow
        to creation's still-accelerating
        end tables and corner shelves
But not to space where life cannot be born
        because what is
        is only what is seen

Startling as it seems . . .

Little Black Box

There are many many more dead Universes—
Cast-offs and flash plastic
The cost of cosmic arbitrage
There and done—and no sense mourning
        such illimitable losses
        such damned, discarded futures
Never a funeral more poorly attended!

All along
        I don the robes of healers
        tending to the countless casualties
Never once without the susurrus
        of rippling moth-wings folding
        and unfolding everywhere about me
Moth-shadows falling and forbidding even
        air, a suffocating shroud, they were
Here before memory
        and frayed at the ends
        into strings and theories of strings
        cut clean with an atom-thin blade
Held by no hand
        a murder—like all—
        committed by the witness.

Star Trek Liberal
(In memoriam E.C.B.)

This is a better world
        I could be drinking, unshaven, waiting for a broken tooth to leave me
        or kill me but I don't do ruin the way, say
        Bukowski did ruin
Instead I watch and watch a perfect show, the canon of unreasonable
        expectations, beginning age five in '66
        (Spock: like a door opening and closing again)
        closing at eight in '69, and it's That
Which Survives.

I'm crying, and fetal on the inside
        and I'm watching these old episodes in the Memory Alpha archives
        (In this mirror, mirror universe they call it "Netflix") and godammit
        I want the better world aboard the Enterprise.

Aboard. On board. On the boards. On the floorboards.
Easy to forget how just a Hollywood set.

I know it can't be Federation space out here,
        not yet, but at least I can wish
        for that tricameral mind—
         not the Medusan-ugly,
        Freudian Forbidden Planet thing
But the action wedded to compassion bounded by logic thing:
        the captain, doctor, science officer
        the all-three we need the becoming of,
        as close to trinity as Jews like me (and two of the three) should ever be.

This is a better world—for one thing, the kind of
        mortal wounds that have put an end to some friends of mine
        always sewn shut in an hour's time
A five-year-old needs to know
        this is real

Little Black Box

The eight-year-old with the exploding father
    already knows better.

I'm crying, and fetal today because Erik
    whose brain, flooded in blood was not replaceable
And could not
    1) be placed in a durable android body
    2) have its consciousness blown into a gold glowing bubble of glass, or
    3) become the controller of a planetary power system

He was an avowed Star Trek Liberal, and we agreed this meant
    salvation by machinery
    resurrection into abundance
    and a limitless heaven of field trips across the unknown universe,
    on five-year missions
    of pet projects
    and whimsical what-ifs
    and the end at last of curiosity's unscratchable itch
Confession: we were never quite sure how happy this would make us.

And in this weightless calculation we were wont to leave out
    Klingons, Romulans and galactic space amoebae
    phaser-proof frisbee parasites,
    and the cornucopic planet-eater, inter alia
Remember the Lights of Zetar? They caused the brain to hemorrhage
    so I have to wonder how much better off
    Erik would be right now
But the good and bad guys always do stand out
    in stark relief
    like Manichaean deities
    like chiaroscuro
    dark on bright:
The grayscale color scheme of Bele and Lokai's final
    battlefield.

I stopped watching but not crying
    and I now remember why: the last
    thing that we talked about, right before I
    went northwest, was

Nazis in Virginia, Sweet Jesus, Nazis—
no poseurs chanting death to Zeon,
but real Nazis, here this century
here last week
—is this really happening?—
We wondered together
        and they might as well have been
        the Klingons,
        so derealized we were
        and for sure: no lines of black and white were blurred
        we knew we were the Federation.

But somewhere you and I diverged
        and maybe I regret it . . .
You said *Klingons* might be on the verge of folding,
        nearly in retreat
I said *Nazis*, they're just getting started
        Beer Hall putsches, all of that
I'm so sorry that I might have changed your mind
        you once said all philosophers are either
        builders or destroyers;
        you were still inclined to sew silk purses
        and I went full-on Shiva with the pigs

You ran right into the Lights of Zetar
        just three or four days later
Taken down, like all the scholars, loving knowledge, knowing
        maybe more than you could bear
Then comes a question in the form of pain,
        behind my sternum
        moving up
        and cut off in my throat, still unanswered . . .
        did we—did I—throw killing shade
        on a photon-hungry Star Trek Liberal's dreaming?

Or did you—as one last injustice
        grave but full of hope and irony—
        have to leave us right before
        the best of all possible reboots?

S. Mia Ling

...and if a ghost should meet a ghost...

at the Oregon beach, at Coos Bay,
where at three in the afternoon
vapor still hangs heavy,
and human shapes disappear

into the white shroud. where
bodies of sea creatures lie
fractured; arms and legs and
severed crowns of jelly fish tossed

like glittering scat upon the brown-
washed sand, transparent and soft
with that sometimes purple viscosity.
where the gray ocean sings in its several voices—

the lighter one, frivolous with
the petulant hiss and suck of waves,
froth fleecing the shore, against the backdrop
of the obsessive incessant throat-

throttled, booming bass that
comes from far-off quakes of middle
sea. and a muter voice, muffled—
footsteps of the dead
shuffling through sand,

whose grains are as multitudinous
as stars, exploding into infinity . . .
here, the high dunes and scissoring grass,
the brumous sky, and the carcasses of wood

. . . would they embrace? or merely salute?
feeling an easy comfort
in this vast empty space,
sharing it with only

a dog

and two strangers . . .

Effluvia

Whenever was water washed like sheets of glass?
Watching through blinders, we peer past
antediluvian hours blurred forward
and back, like the splash of a great
tide, churning memories outside in.

I have hard digging in these waters
smoking out the source of sound,
finding rust where there was wood,
splinters where there were bones,
vapor where there was sound.

We are gliding on the lake, waveless.
The gray green hours slick with times past
below the listless surface, shagreen blues.
The abacus clicks its numbers, true or false
and we stiffen, listening, trying to decipher
the random mutilation of our times.

Remotely past, there was a time when all was clear.
I could see for miles beyond, and know
what it was like to be loved, to be kissed,
feel the burn of life and see only clean pearls of white
round beads so perfect in their originality.

Sentence me, penitent for this
frailty, a poorly made step   oh
indeed, we are anything but what we were
those poorly made swimmers come afloat
like drifting sea toss

And know, know so well, that once I was
the thing swimming to shore, leaping in the wind,
as swift as a sky, a tree, anything that was good,
a treasure of ducats, muscle and teeth shined
into a matrimony of hope and youth.

Little Black Box

How to account for every moment passed
with every article spent I see those minutes,
false and multiplied into a life, my life

My life inside a bottle
floating
unmade garments as loose as a madman's mind.

A Photograph of the Painter Painting the Two Fridas

You sit there, palette in hand,
staring at the two mirrors
of yourself, a painter
> so placid
> so decent
> so normal

while depicting the soon-to-be
venomous twin selves in self-
mutilation, dissection.

In this photo we have
not doubles, but triples,
the three of them a case study:
the painter with mindless
schizophrenia
waving the sheer curtains
of her personality,
> the jazz
> of her smile,
> one tooth

set on the other. The suite
of endless ruffled skirts,
fringes like wild veronicas,
trifling the staccato of her
anguish, beating solo
against itself.

Suffer the spear jammed through
your stomach, the walrus tusk
and the silken haunting
and that pair of cherry lips,
> oh darling,
> two of you
> too daring,
> two much,

the pulse of one hand holding
your own, as if in affirmation
of your twin self, the endless
reflection pinging light,
the red corpuscles oozing
unwillingly transfusing,
exsanguinating
the other,
the prim giver of blood
       in blood-stained white,
       the peasant, brown
       and accepting,
her single brow and moustache
stiffening like pig bristles
having eaten the cloven heart.

What will save you –
    the candy
      of your marriage –
    the hat
of your cheating husband?
Paintings and endless images tryst.
Your insecurities add
no security—they
can't be stored up or
locked like securities
in the bank. Look!

overhead, the clouds
thrown up like proffered doves wings
are cooing a tornado, cycling
round your head. We know the ice
of your igloo. One of you smirks
ready to dance moonlight.
The painter has no pity,
no sweet smelling
devices, hooligans

her invention, down the other
        through straws
        of pastiche.
        The third,
        another other
        half observes.

Persephone and the Girls Club

"Only six seeds of a pomegranate, are you joking?" she scoffs.

"Six very, very, very small seeds," I rejoin. "Hardly even noticeable."

"Those gods are idiots. Don't they know she'd be starving after a year in that cold, fucking dark hell-hole of a place? How was she even still alive?"

"Idiots, those gods!"

"On the other hand, six seeds is six seeds. And isn't there a saying, *a whole world in a grain of mustard*?" She has never been consistent.

But I agree, "Or *a universe in an atom*?"

"So even though they were very small seeds, they encompassed the whole world of pomegranates in their being?" she asks carefully.

"Yes, a kind of synecdoche. The seed representing all fruiting."

"DNA is very small too, isn't it?"

"But long. They say the helix from one cell, if unwound, could reach from here to the moon."

"So thin it's invisible, but stretching out forever!"

"Yes," I say, "Lots of little things affecting lots of big things. And because of that, we have winter and equinox and all that shit for half the year, every single year. Snow, ice, falling down, car accidents, broken hips, busted pipes, avalanches and carbon monoxide poisoning. All because of silly old Persephone and her six pomegranate seeds."

"Are you sure it was six?"

"Whatever..."

"But in some places, like Hawaii, it's always fudge-delicious, warm and toasty, and never rains and double even triple rainbows in the sky every day," she sighs dreamily.

"Impossible! You're mixing metaphors now. No rain, no rainbows."

"In Hawaii they get rainbows from waterfalls."

"Still, I'm never going to eat a pomegranate seed in my whole entire life!" I declare.

"Me neither. Not even if it was the last pomegranate seed on earth," she agrees.

Persephone is the cause of our yearly misery, the cold wintry dark period, because she couldn't leave those pomegranate seeds alone. I hate her.

The deep voice behind us makes us jump. He has a beautifully embroidered bag with gleaming red seeds so luscious they look like jewels.

"How many, young ladies?" he asks with a charming smile.

He himself is handsome as a god, in a black velvet cloak and silver helmet, atop a chariot drawn by impatient stallions, while the river of sticks flows behind him.

The Love We Bore Him, Elegy to Conrad Balliet

September, 2018

I had received an email detailing Conrad's accident, his paralysis and subsequent inability to swallow, his refusal to have a feeding tube.
That night he appeared to me in a dream. He was a young boy.
We were in a room in an unknown school, the room suffused with light.

He was so young, his schoolboy shirt unlined
I spoke to him
        he did not answer me
He had a pencil in his hand and his fist was clenched
around it, like a pencil sharpener
He was busy, absorbed in something I could not see,
I tried to catch a glance
        he did not answer me

We were silent together, two children, and my eyes
        were awestruck by our quiet dance,
        solemn and alone

As we sat there, the bones of his face changed and he became the Conrad
that I knew
The old Conrad, with the profile of his Adam's apple pronounced and clear,
        searching through his mounds of books,
        turning his head so he could better hear,
I saw his lips move, the words washing in and out
        garbled, without meaning—
        a shout, but of despair

As I looked again, a halo richly woven,
        wavered above the space where his face had been
And an unseen mouth spoke with fairy lightness,
        a Gaelic lilt
        reading to a higher meaning,
        resonant beyond my hearing

His whole body was drifting,
        away toward the school room window, truly
        breath became a hum, a drone, a buzz
        and in his fist, my heart clenched,
        resigned
        to the clouds of death seeping in
        as time crept out the crevices

All his ages mashed at once together,
the separate lumps fighting destiny
        schoolboy
        school master
        naughty imp
        scalawag even
        wit, and poet

The lover
Ever the lover

I called, I spoke,
he could not answer
There was only a white glaze
and a smile
floating in the room, uncatchable

Herbert Woodward Martin

A Monk's Prayer and Blessing

let there always be rhythm
let there always be melody
in the blood. let it ruminate
in the marrow of the bones,
and restrained by the skin.
let ears be aware of time
let the skin be aware of
knowledge let the fingers
be aware of all motion,
let them be instruments
of choosing and what the
Lord himself calls:

The pulse of life.

Julie L. Moore

Opening Day
with two lines from Hemingway

April showers surged as the temperature slipped
    down its red slide into the cold
        pool of dawn. And the creek roiled
            as it filled and overspilled

its banks. Then thunder
    spoke words of snow
        surreal as paradox,
            as the sight of beauty

just before death,
    petals of the white rose
        filleting the loin of air
            as they fall to the ground.

I stood on my deck, amazed,
    watched flakes fluttering
        and an old man standing in the wild
            stream as it lunged

through his legs. He kept plunging
    his hands into the dark waters,
        grasping at something
            elusive, like a shadow, or a dream,

snatching nothing but a cramp.
    So he shook his left hand with zeal,
        as if to unhook
            a leech embedded in his muscle.

And he talked to himself aloud, hailing
    Mary, then wondering,
        What would the great DiMaggio do?
            like he was looking for inspiration.

Little Black Box

Then he turned,
>craned his neck,
>>cast his body so it arced
>>>like a fishing line

over the water, and with him,
>my eyes strained to catch
>>*the great erect tail*
>>>*slicing through the dark.*

Shadow of Death

You can't forget the grave
once you've stared down its well
of despair, pondering its promise

of reprieve, a permanent stay of pain's stubborn
execution. I wish I would, of course.
I wish I would not see myself

in silhouettes drawn by the dark lines
of disease, in figures like Roth's
Millicent Kramer who swallowed

all her pills to extinguish the flames
of affliction, to leave Everyman
to join everyone who'd gone before her.

I wish I would see myself
only in the resurrected versions,
like impatiens, choked by a string

of rainless days, breaking free,
unfurling their pink tongues
beneath the burst of silver clouds,

or that man in the news who awoke—
Praise the Lord!—cancerless,
yawning and stretching while the grim reaper

looked the other way. Oh, I know
I'm like them, like Lazarus who rose
to the challenge of a new life. But I can't seem

to cut off the shadow
of that death. No, it stays with me,
nipping at my heels,

following me wherever I go.

Aftershock

People may be able to go much longer without a pulse than the 20 minutes previously believed. The capnograph, which measures carbon dioxide being expelled from the mouth of the patient, can tell rescuers when further efforts at cardiopulmonary resuscitation . . . should be continued.

—WALL STREET JOURNAL, May 17, 2011

*I'm a regular guy. I happened to die
at the right place at the right time,*
said Howard Snitzer after he was revived.

Ninety-six minutes he spent without a pulse
lying in front of a grocery store while Mayo medics
worked on him, using a capnograph

to gauge how his lungs clung to longer life.

In that hour & a half, did his soul wander
down the banks of the Acheron River,
chat with Charon, who refused to ferry him

to the other side, immediately knowing, as he did,
that Howard was neither dead man
nor tragic hero, no Aeneas, for example, bearing

golden branch & the burden of a nation's destiny?

When asked what he was doing there,
did Howard shrug his shoulders
& shove his hands into his disembodied

pockets, then jangle those immaterial
coins the cashier gave him
after purchasing milk, bread, & eggs?

How impatient did Charon grow

as he counted like strikes of a clock the echoes
of defibrillator shocks—twelve in all—
rocking his usually steady boat?

Is this the story Charon now tells every spirit
he takes for a ride—how the water
throbbed beneath his feet, how in the end,

he rubbed his eyes in disbelief?

In a parallel universe

which some physicists say may exist,
perhaps the husband actually asks
for forgiveness, head bowed,
confessing his offenses,
giving them their proper names—
this being one alternative
on a quantum scale that doesn't mean
how it sounds—not epic, but *small*.
Then again, when she stares at memory's
polychromatic walls, she thinks of Pollock's
full-bodied swirls, how they imitate
the same geometry of galaxies,
& wonders whether her existence
preceded its essence, or the other way around,
while she walks along the floors of her future,
the night sky, her roof,
Earth's lone moon, her window,
God's good stars, particles
of light in the only life she knows.

The first time I saw a shooting star,

I was 42, and the world was busy casting
its orange shadow onto the surface of the moon.

The red eye of a plane was blinking
as it slipped beneath Orion's Belt,

the rumble of the engine too far away to hear.

Icicles, invisible in the dark,
crackled in the near-zero air,

Splitting their grips,
tinkling like glass as tips reached

The sleet-topped snow below.

The wind was still, asleep in its cloudless bed.
The wafer of wonder crisp on my tongue.

My prayer, simple,
spoken aloud like the soft call of an owl:

O God, maker of heaven and earth, heal my husband.

Then the flame, light years old,
streamed through the sky.

And I was as skeptical as you are now,
my faith in any true goodness

eclipsed by the pain in my life.

But I tell you, it happened like this:
visible as the disappearing moon,

the light, long-awaited, arrived.

Prufrock in My Backyard

I see him this morning
in the long, wet grass, dandelion hanging
from his mouth like a question mark.

He is visible despite the mist
that still shrouds the house
after last night's storm, like a ball,

rolled through. He's rubbing
his back against the peach tree
like a cat might chafe a chair,

inhaling the peachy perfume,
looking rather conspicuous, really,
in his hundred-year-old coat and tie,

holding an empty teacup,
sporting a bald spot
yes, in the middle of his hair.

I don't know if somehow I conjured him
to appear—maybe turned last night's attendant
toad into him when I stroked its neck

and kissed its slick nose?—but there he is,
back from the dead like you know who,
picking up where he left off—

indeed, virtually hopeless,
so easily distracted as he is by the voices
of song sparrow, robin, crow.

Robert Paschell

If the Sun Is a White Witch

the moon is its bright-eyed familiar
a Cheshire Cat of phases
perched on an empty bough
its whiskery light tickling Terra's flanks
its long gravitational tail stirring waters
styling the oceans with tides

Archaeopteryx

Gotcher lizard, gotcher bird.
One has scales, the other flits.
But by this hybrid put an asterisk.
Long time ago it hopped on sticks.
We call it "archaeopteryx."

Whoever thought that skin of leather
would yield a wind-puff fluffy feather?
That from the skin of lizard innate
would spring a barbuled structure pinnate.

If petro imprints scribe a Braille,
whilst separating leaves of shale
in rocky cave, in earthen nook—
like leafing through the pages
of a living history book.
In stony grot, by lamplight's gleam,
some German miners glimpsed
the fossil blueprint of a creature
in-between—twixt sky and heath.

A lizard with wings?
A bird with teeth?

Just one—no phalanx culled from day trips—
the archaeopteryx was ripped from rocky matrix
to inspire
phoenix-fueled musings on the nature
of Nature's metamorphic funeral pyre.
Now fallen into streambed, now soaring
ever higher—
past paleo pale.
And so I've spun the thread
and fanned the tale.
And I dare say tis no fib—
thar's feathers in the flight of words
and teeth in this pen's nib.

Untitled

Should the US and Chinese rovers
ever bump into each other on Mars
and wish to converse, would they need a translator?

Probably not, as they both speak fluid machine,
the mother tongue of function.

After exchanging pleasantries:
"Fancy meeting you here!"
"It's a small rust-brown world."
I would like to imagine them
drilling down on the subject of soil samples.
Taking the measure of the scanty atmosphere.
Swapping data in an ancient riverbed
like two eagle-eyed wampum-trading frontier scouts.

The Chinese rover making a crack about the ubiquity of redness.
Its American counterpart attended by its Tinkerbelle-like drone.
Its dual-rotor, pint-sized, orbital, Jiminy Cricket familiar,
gaining hard won purchase in the tenuous Martian air.

The Hidden Valley

And now with arm outstretched
and palm greased with peanuts
I am trying to lure the chipmunk
of sleep from his plain-faced burrow
that he might show his sly hoodwinking
face and leave a cheek pouch full of
moonbeams in the hidden valley of my mind

David A. Petreman

What To Do With a Dead Angel

Dig a hole in the back yard.
The authorities will never believe
What you have to say anyway.

Wrap him like a Pharaoh,
Send him down the river
With no material possessions.

Try to revive him,
Move his arms up and down,
See if he takes flight.

Prop him up on the couch,
Fold his hands into yours,
Talk about miracles.

Stare into the distance
And think about why
He died in the first place.

Valentina Ranaldi-Adams

Proxima b citizens
report a UFO—
Earth Ship One

two hearts
un-beating as one—
vampire love

moon walk—
Earthlight Sonata plays
inside my helmet

I have the legs
for trick-or-treating . . .
spider veins

streaming now—
Captain Ultraviolet
Versus the Virus Menace

black widow spider . . .
her mate's hourglass time
is running out

Janeal Turnbull Ravndal

All Things New

Sun splashes no same pattern on this floor
Both waves and words have no exact encore.
No two of anything be truly twin;
Time fingerprints each cell or smile or stain.
Fine wine, the copy page, an organ tone
We can approximate, but never clone –
Much less a creature or a sunset hue
Which each eternal now is wholly new.
What seems identical's but true illusion.
No wind will ever match this current motion.
Like waves, our words have no precise encore.
Sun splashes no same pattern on this floor.

Meeting for Worship

You can get there from anywhere.

Put in the center of the patched fir floor:
        An orange peel
        Or a bowl of water
        Or this small blue rug.

In the real world

In this room for instance
There is always an arc
Waiting for us to add the colors
With our broken crayons.

Anything taken seriously will do
        Including hilarity
        Or Ecclesiastes
        Or this small blue rug.

Put anything there in the center
Or for that matter
Pay attention to the patched fir floor.

Whatever occurs to you will do
To connect us:
        A song
        Or all the unreported rapes
        Or this small blue rug.

You can get there from anywhere.

Visitor

When death steps out of the shadow
with or without a songbird on her
shoulder, I want to stop my
knitting, to smile or bow
perhaps, and trustfully,
in the manner of a child
soon to cross a busy street,
take her outstretched hand.

When death rings my doorbell
I want to answer, not grudgingly,
not complaining that the cake is still
in the oven or fussing about the right
gloves and scarf for the trip, just wiping
soapy hands on my apron, still humming.

Even if it is a long walk single file, and
whether I am still awake or sleeping
with only strangers round my bed
and no words left in the world,
I want to meet her in good
humor, open to the simple
truth of my ending.

Barbara A. Sabol

cocooned still dreaming of flight

immense heaven—
feeling the tug
of other galaxies

red moon
alien insects scurry
in the spotlight

planetarium—
in search of
a safer world

Field Notes from the Moons of Mars

Spring Equinox

Off-planet disorientation, afloat between ice and melt on the fringe
of Phobos, innermost moon of the red planet. In my head, I can travel
anywhere. Spring now on Mars a deserted landscape: light, shadow/ice cap,
sea bed. Back on my fragile planet white wetness etches the world.
Crystalline. Hushed as here. No sound but my blood pumping, radio static,
wind rattle through a mobile of stars.

Spectrometer aimed into the measurable space between me and Mars.
Detecting signs of life: datum: methane, a plume! Datum: vapor cloud,
Datum: weather patterns robust. Through the oxidized dust, a dazzle of stars—
silver scales of fish heads, bobbing, mouths opening and opening
in the thin, indifferent air.

And dust, clouds of it everywhere. Downy coating on my skin, silting
my eyes into slits. Henna hair. Antler velvet. I am swallowing cosmic dust.
I am cosmic dust.

* * *

Summer Solstice

Glacial in full Martian equatorial summer. Foil-wrapped at the dash,
my gangle-winged craft set on *cruise*. Last whip around the planet;
three orbits a day. Dizzy drunk on the gyre. Addicted to the spin,
the luminous blur. Throttle back, watch a debris cloud stream past.
Contents: bits of satellite latticework; neon paint flakes; one glove
reaching. (*Loneliness dangerous.*) A wrench.

This once, the seasons align—my fossil world verdant, this other
baked in the great solar kiln. Wild flowers riot in my earthly garden,
violets choke the roses—bruise bouquet. No blooms in space,
except what sprouts in my brain. Hazard quotient: incalculable.
Solar wind velocity: low. Geomagnetic activity: off the scale.

* * *

Little Black Box

Autumn Equinox

Eyes adjusting, off-key shades of red—arroyo, tomato, match head—
as Mars spins away from the sun. The measured seasonal turn.

On my fossil world, gauzy flakes froth the crimson remains
in my back yard. Akron, an abstraction. Carols piped into the white air.
Imagine ivory window light—shapes pass, arms reach, hands gesture.
Mars now closest to my own blue planet. Gorged with light—
scoped through the naked trees, a glowing gala apple.

In space, a titanium broad-brushed cosmos. A world caked in feldspar dust.
Strands of white lights wink in a fine-gauged mesh of blackness.
Now auroras streak across Mars's skies! Cerulean waves bathe my eyes.
I remember the salt water, lapping, foam at my ankles, the eventual
plunge.

* * *

Winter Solstice

A full Martian year, riding the orbit of this doomed moon, pulled ever closer
to its parent, locked in; gravity irresistible. On earth, trillium and dogwood,
rushing rivers. Azaleas bud against white shutters. *Don't look down!*
Indigo shadow of Deimos, sister moon, hoops above; larger, farther
from the parent planet. She will orbit on and on while Phobos whirls
an intimate distance from the red orb, spirals in, a shining ring, infinite spin.

while I launch back into the blue: a nimbus of white silk parachutes me
through clouds, wren chatter, dew. Far above, moon mountains and canyons
will dissolve—string of pearls, band of jewels, always a mystery, beautiful,
dutiful, circling in the left-over light. Earth spills upward: emerald canopy,
shingle-glisten roof tops, kestrels over corn fields. Balconies of light. Singing.

Myrna Stone

The Third Spring After

Their animals
are birthing again:
this morning the cow
delivered herself of a calf
with a fifth leg
growing from its belly.
They stunned
the misshapen head
with a bat
before drawing
the knife.

The hill
behind their barn
is honeycombed now
with shallow pits.
Soon they'll have to bury
in the pasture.

Come dusk,
they'll gather on the porch
to search the sky
while insects scour
the rising moon.
Perhaps this
will be the night
they take the gun
from the kitchen shelf,
the last two bullets
from the teapot.

The Swimmer

Too late he registers his error
as the blue ball, that buoyant sphere
of air toward which he strokes, bobs away,
surely as lost to him now as he is to his wife
and sons lolling on the beach, each of whom
appears to him blindly or willfully oblivious.
He floats for a moment, slack and breathless,
flotsam on the ebbing tide of the fathomless
Gulf waters off Naples, Florida, a man who
on any other day could be found soaping up
his van, making love to his wife, counseling
his children, a man who carries out the trash
and wipes down the tub after he bathes, who
subscribes even here, in the absence of hope,
to the resurrective power of muscle, its holy
grit, who, turning into the swell, will not
open his mouth again until the mouth
that would swallow him opens.

A Thin Place

A mesmerizing location where heaven and earth overlap

No order or law we know explains the consort
of lure and lore, or why a bridge which soars

four dozen feet above a gorge in Dumbarton,
Scotland, compels dogs both small and large

to jump its parapets to their breakage or death.
What causes it, one local offers, *is the heady*

*scent of animals below which drives dogs quite
mad.* . . . Mad or not, three hundred have leapt

into the hushed plush crevasse through which
the Overtoun burn wends its green stitchery,

having drawn dozens of them, already unsound
and spellbound, into its watery depths to drown.

Others, airborne from parapets closer to entry
points onto the bridge, find a more temporary

rest in the gossamery ferns along the burn's
mossy berm. *Our resident spirit here spurs*

them on, happy to steward their mortal race,
another local says. That specter, a Mrs. Grace

White, her name the only import given her
at birth and marriage, is most often referred

to now as the *White Lady of Overtoun House*
who, for three decades, refused to renounce

widow's weeds as she mourned her beloved.
She appears irregularly, ghosting her leaded

casements overlooking the gorge, and, less
often, drifting in her fallow garden's gorse,

though she and the dogs, in the way of all such
thin places, remain aloof and predictably mute.

George Percy, Leader of the Virginia Colonists on Their Desperation During the Starving Time
James Towne, Late Winter, 1610

No ship saves us from this our ghastly winnowing.
Today, in three communal kettles, we boil the last
of our leather aprons, our fine saddlery trappings,

and boots harvested from the bodies of our frozen
dead. Thus shall we fill our bellies as we must lest
we sup on air. Our dogs, cats, horses, and vermin

of every sort, we have already eaten. The savages,
who for months have encircled our palisade, taunt
us today with a creel of dried corn which ravishes

our common senses, as it lies just beyond the range
of our muskets. A fortnight ago, Hugh Price, lately
of Lutterworth, and newly bereft of his mind, raged

in the marketplace that if there were truly a just God
He would not suffer creatures whom He had made
and framed to endure such miseries. And, indeed,

a mere day and a half later, in the woods nearby,
he met his Maker, slain by Powhatans as brutally
outside these walls as famine hath slain us inside.

Others less addled have endured the selfsame fate
as hunger compelled them to risk foraging at dusk
beyond the gates for moss, pine bark, and snakes.

And one other, whom I shall not herewith name,
a colonist depraved beyond all reason, murdered
his young wife as she lay fast asleep beside him,

Little Black Box

then cut out the child in her womb and threw it
in the river. Hours later, after butchering his wife,
he scored, salted, and potted what he could not eat.

We hanged him by the thumbs, with iron weights
upon his feet, a quarter of an hour before he would
confess the same. For such heinous crimes, fraught

with the Devil's own bile, we burned him alive.
We who are left have not murdered. Nor do we
dream of it. Yet our brains buzz like beehives

each time we resurrect a body from this foul earth.
We beg God for forgiveness, and believe that He
offers it to us even as we sin anew in our cursed

extremity. When the leather is gone, we shall go
about stewing what is left of the young wife's flesh
in a broth of roots, herbs, and well-powdered bone.

Orison to an Owl

      It is, finally, your voice, isolate
and desirous, that draws us to this dusk

          of woodland and bramble, this locus
of shadow beneath the walnut's arc of light

          and leaf. Yet here, too, you are nothing
if not spirit, a presence that compels us

          to silence, to our knees to sift the earth
for talismans and signs, to embrace

          darkness, and come the sun, find no
relief. . . . O animus of evening, O shim

          of horn and feather, of talon and beak,
you who have launched a thousand myths,

          what oblation, what felter of flesh
and bristle, must we offer now?

At Wethersfield Burial Ground

Leafwork and bonework is want
tangible as the antiquated diction
tourists trace from the slate stones
on the hill at the back of the church.

Tangible as the antiquated diction
a maple in the autumn air is burning
on the hill at the back of the church
branch by branch down to its essence.

A maple in the autumn air is burning
red and red in the late morning light
branch by branch down to its essence
of pith and sap, vein and marrow.

Red and red in the late morning light
bodies go down painted and emptied
of pith and sap, vein and marrow.
Leafwork and bonework is want.

Steve Van Allen

October night
stray cat less
than a shadow

weeping cypress
a silent cry
in the forest

Saga of the Fruit Bats
by Steve Van Allen and *Linda Z. Chernick*

Sundown, we fly by the thousands
over a beach by the eastern sea
We rule the night sky
We drink the gods' nectar
every fig and flower
guavas and Raja mangos
There is enough for all

We have flown each night
since the world was young
Great leatherback turtles were old
when we appeared
We were here before the Chola[1]
ancient India
Before Mylapore[2] became Chennai
Sundown, we fly by the thousands

> *Big moon rising*
> *Appetite so huge she*
> *Tries to eat the sky*

---

1. Chola Kingdom 3rd century BC
2. Mylapore (means butterfly in Tamil) 1st century BC

MJ Werthman White

The Ten Thousand Things

In the Tao, ten thousand was thought of as such an unimaginably large number that it came to stand for the equivalent of all of reality.

Most agree that at the end of a long life, Lao Tzu
found himself no longer enamored of the material,
except for the company of his ox. Who would not
appreciate a warm, breathing presence, capable
of bearing old bones on a final trip, a large, stolid,
silent animal to take you where you want to go,
never interrupting your thoughts? Old myself,
I could see choosing ox over Honda any day.

At the last minute, almost out of town,
the philosopher was persuaded by a gatekeeper
to write down his thoughts on the ten thousand things.
You read the Tao. It's not my intent to summarize,
put together a powerpoint, make it easy for you.
I only want to say the universe may be infinite,
your computer hold five hundred gigabytes,
but ten thousand is more than enough to name a world.

Bigger is not better. Listen to Lao.

The Shagbark

After the rain the windows this summer morning are
fogged with ghostly condensation, as though the storms
thundering through last night's fitful dreams had lifted
a yard-full of displaced spirits and flung them against the glass,

spirits left homeless when, instead of hickory nuts, our towering
shagbark ended likely her centennial year hurling widow-makers,
each huge branch snapping, letting go without warning, hitting
the ground where a yellow dog and two clueless humans

happened to be elsewhere. Sooner or later luck runs out-
the tree had to go and, yesterday, went, leaving behind
today's inconsolable wraiths. The arborist pointed out
the heartwood was gone, consumed by fungus, by insects,

by rapacious time, leaving behind a fragile, unstable dowager
with anger issues. So we mourn along with her attendant
spirits, knowing well what it means to lose heart, to be
broken, what it feels like to have to finally let go.

Afterword

Tribute to Conrad Balliet

The Tower Poets remember cold evenings gathered around Conrad Balliet's wood stove, sharing poetry and enjoying Conrad's warm homemade raisin bread with Irish butter. Conrad was a lifelong Yeats scholar and sometimes read a work by his favorite poet. We include the following speculative selection as a tribute to him.

Song of the Wandering Aengus
by W. B. Yeats

I went out to the hazel wood,
Because a fire was in my head,
And cut and peeled a hazel wand,
And hooked a berry to a thread;
And when white moths were on the wing,
And moth-like stars were flickering out,
I dropped the berry in a stream
And caught a little silver trout.

When I had laid it on the floor
I went to blow the fire aflame,
But something rustled on the floor,
And someone called me by my name:
It had become a glimmering girl
With apple blossom in her hair
Who called me by my name and ran
And faded through the brightening air.

Though I am old with wandering
Through hollow lands and hilly lands,
I will find out where she has gone,
And kiss her lips and take her hands;
And walk among long dappled grass,
And pluck till time and times are done
The silver apples of the moon,
The golden apples of the sun.

Contributor Biographies

Kathy B. Austin has published in the *Writing Path 1* anthology (University of Iowa Press), *Northern Appalachian Review, Weber—The Contemporary West, Buddhist Poetry Journal, Flights, Poppy Road Review, Glide,* and *Mock Turtle Zine.* She has received awards from the Dayton Metro Library, Iowa Poetry Day Association, and the Paul Laurence Dunbar Memorial Competition. Over the years, many of her poems have been aired on Conrad's Corner, WYSO 91.3. Kathy is now a retired graphic designer from Dayton, Ohio and describes herself as a Buddhist half hippie tree-hugger who enjoys biking, hiking, art, and gardening. Her poetry is informed by linear and spiritual connectedness, nature, and the difficulty in remembering we are all one. She listens to the words of trees and talks to crows and any other creatures who will lend her an ear.

Steve Broidy is an emeritus professor of education at both Missouri State University and Wittenberg University. He is the editor/contributor of *From the Tower: Poetry in Honor of Conrad Balliet,* and author of the chapbooks *Earth Inside Them* and *Necessary Deceptions* (all Main Street Rag Press). He also authored *A Case for Kindness: A New Look at the Teaching Ethic* (Myers Education Press). With his wife, Susan, a sculptor, he resides in rural Southwest Ohio.

Anna Cates is a graduate of Indiana State University (M.A. English and Ph.D. Curriculum & Instruction/English), and National University (M.F.A. Creative Writing). She teaches college writing and literature and graduate education online. Her poetry awards include First Place in Indiana State University's *Arion Poetry Contest,* First Place in Ohio Poetry Day's *Welcome Aboard Contest,* First Place in Ohio Poetry Day's *Haiku for Betty Contest,* and Ohio Poetry Day's *Evan Lodge Workshop Contest Award.* Her poetry has been nominated for Best of the Net, the Pushcart Prize, and the Dwarf Stars, Elgin, and Rhysling awards. Her books include: *The Meaning of Life* (Cyberwit Press), *The Frog King* (Cyberwit Press), *The Darkroom* (Prolific Press), *The Golem & the Nazi* (Red Moon Press), *The Journey* (Wipf & Stock), *Love in the Time of Covid* (Wipf & Stock), and *The Poison Tree: A Peace Play* (Wipf & Stock). She resides in Wilmington, Ohio, with her beautiful kitties, Freddie and Fifi.

Linda Z. Chernick has been a writer since producing columns for her Springfield, Ohio high school newspaper. After turning her hand to poetry, she produced a chapbook, *The Turning: Poems of Love, Loss and Renewal*, which has been used in a course on grief. Other poems have been published in *Pages Literary Journal* and *Ripples*, a Yellow Springs, Ohio publication. One of her poems was selected for a holiday-themed mailing sent to 400 recipients nationwide. She currently has two poems in a book in process on poets writing about poems and poetry.

Ed Davis has immersed himself in writing and contemplative practices since retiring from college teaching. *Time of the Light,* a poetry collection, was released by Main Street Rag Press in 2013. His latest novel, *The Psalms of Israel Jones* (West Virginia University Press 2014), won the Hackney Award for an unpublished novel in 2010. Many of his stories, essays, and poems have appeared in anthologies and journals such as *Leaping Clear, Slippery Elm, Hawaii Pacific Review,* and *Bacopa Literary Review*. He lives with his wife in the bucolic village of Yellow Springs, Ohio, where he bikes, hikes, meditates, and writes an occasional poetry column for the *Yellow Springs News*.

Cathryn Essinger is the author of five books of poetry—most recently *The Apricot and the Moon* and *Wings, Or Does the Caterpillar Dream of Flight?*, from Dos Madres Press. Her poems have appeared in *Poetry, The Southern Review, The New England Review, The Antioch Review, Rattle, River Styx, Ecotone, Terrain, Calyx,* and other journals. They have been nominated for Pushcarts and Best of the Net, featured on *The Writer's Almanac*, and reprinted in *American Life in Poetry*. She was Ohio's Poet of the Year in 2005 when she received an Ohio Arts Council Individual Excellence Award. She is a long-standing member of the Greenville Poets. She lives in Troy, Ohio where she raises Monarch butterflies.

Sharon H. Frost earned a master's degree in criminology from the University of Cincinnati and resides in Wilmington, OH. She is a world traveler, having visited every continent and 141 countries and islands, including Antarctica. Her poetry has appeared in *Otoliths*, *Haiku Canada*, and *Pages Literary Journal*.

David Lee Garrison: The poetry of David Lee Garrison has been read by Garrison Keillor on "The Writer's Almanac" and featured by Ted Kooser in his column, "American Life in Poetry." Named Ohio Poet of the Year in 2014, his most recent book is *Light in the River* (Dos Madres Press).

Patrick S. Gentile: The late **Patrick S. Gentile** (1946–2014) was a physician and faithful member of the Tower Poets and Wilmington Writer's Collaborative.

Jennifer Hambrick: A four-time Pushcart Prize and Best of the Net nominee, Jennifer Hambrick is author of *In the High Weeds*, winner of the Stevens Manuscript Award (National Federation of State Poetry Societies); *Joyride* (Red Moon Press), winner of the 2022 Marianne Bluger Book Award from Haiku Canada; and *Unscathed* (NightBallet Press). She was featured by former U.S. Poet Laureate Ted Kooser in *American Life in Poetry*; was appointed the inaugural Artist-in-Residence at historic Bryn Du Mansion, Granville, Ohio. Her awards and prizes include the Sheila-Na-Gig Press Poetry Prize, First Prize in the Haiku Society of America's Haibun Award Competition, First Prize in the 2021 Martin Lucas Haiku Award Competition (U.K.), and other honors from Tokyo's NHK World TV, the Irish Haiku Society, the Haiku Society of America, Haiku Poets of Northern California, the Ohio Poetry Association, and others. A classical musician, public radio broadcaster, multimedia producer, and cultural journalist, Jennifer Hambrick lives in Columbus, Ohio. jenniferhambrick.com.

Artie Isaac is a Yellow Springs area poet and author of *Pandemonia: Poems in Seclusion* (Amazon). More by Artie Isaac is located at PoetryForDogs.com.

Frederic Stuart (Skip) Leeds is a writer, musician, and an Associate Professor of Family Medicine at Wright State University, currently and perpetually living in Yellow Springs, OH. His work is deeply influenced by the Beats, as well as more recent poets. He considers poetry the art of the unexpected obvious. And though a poem might well begin as an inside joke to oneself . . . it's a shame if it never makes good its escape to the outside world. His poems have previously appeared in the *Mock Turtle Zine*, *Blue Skies*, *Ripples*, the *Pages Literary Journal* . . . and somehow, one was even published in a peer-reviewed medical journal!

S. Mia Ling: Out of China into the patulous Midwest, bewitched by the slang, twang, and drawl of the cornfields, the big moon, and buffeted by the seasons. Founder of the Wilmington Writers Collaborative, member of Tower Poets, often heard on WYSO Conrad's Corner poetry minute.

Herbert Woodward Martin finds himself a librettist, having written five libretti while thinking he was doing something else. He has written eleven books of poetry, the last of which, *Sometimes, Say My Name*, won the BLM Award for Poetry in 2021. He is the Paul Laurence Dunbar Laureate Poet for Dayton, Ohio.

Julie L. Moore is author of *Election Day* (Finishing Line Press, 2006), *Slipping Out of Bloom* (WordTech Edition, 2010), *Particular Scandals* (Wipf & Stock, 2013), and *Full Worm Moon* (Wipf & Stock, 2018). Formerly an Ohio resident and member of the Tower Poets, she currently serves as Writing Center Director and Associate Professor of English at Taylor University.

Robert Paschell has been writing poetry for over sixty years. He sells punny t-shirts on the streets of Yellow Springs, Ohio, including one that says: I'M A RHYME-STONED COWBOY!

David A. Petreman is the author of *Candlelight in Quintero* (Dos Madres Press, 2011) and *Francisco in the Days of Exile* (Finishing Line Press, 2007) as well as several books on Chilean writers. He has also translated books by several Chilean poets. Petreman has given some seventy-five poetry readings at universities, libraries, cultural centers and bars. He lives in Milford, Ohio.

Valentina Ranaldi-Adams was born in the USA to parents from Arpino, Italy. She earned a degree in mathematics from the University of Akron and worked as a computer programmer for the Goodyear Tire and Rubber Company. Valentina won a Lit Youngstown 2017 Words Made Visible

Prize, a 2019 Art of Haiku Silver Prize, and was nominated for the 2019, 2020, and 2022 SFPA Dwarfs Stars Speculative Poetry Award. Her work has appeared in many journals, including *Akitsu Quarterly, Cattails, Failed Haiku, Frogpond, Modern Haiku, Ohio Haiku Anthology, Presence*, and *#FemkuMag*.

Janeal Turnbull Ravndal is a retired social worker. With her husband of sixty-four years, Chris, she lived in Quaker educational communities before her 2006 retirement to Yellow Springs, Ohio. In 2004, after her civil disobedience during the U.S. War in Iraq, she spent a week in Philadelphia's federal prison. She reflects on that experience in her Pendle Hill Pamphlet, *A Very Good Week Behind Bars*, and in her full-length poetry collection, *From Parsonage to Prison*.

Barbara A Sabol: Barbara Sabol's fourth poetry collection, *Imagine a Town*, was published in 2020. Her long-form and short-form Japanese poetry has appeared in many journals and anthologies. She is the Associate Editor of *Sheila-Na-Gig* online poetry journal. Her awards include an Individual Excellence Award from the Ohio Arts Council. She teaches poetry workshops for local NE Ohio poetry literary centers. Barbara lives in Akron, Ohio with her husband and wonder dogs.

Myrna Stone is the author of six books of poems, most recently *The Resurrectionist's Diary* (Dos Madres Press, July 2021). A two-time Ohioana Book Award Finalist, her work has appeared in nine anthologies and in over fifty journals including *Poetry, Southwest Review, The Massachusetts Review, Boulevard, Nimrod*, and *River Styx*. She is the recipient of three Ohio Arts Council Individual Excellence Awards, a full fellowship to Vermont Studio Center, the 2001 Ohio Poet of the Year award, and the 2017 New Letters Prize in Poetry. Stone is a founding member of the Greenville Poets, based in Greenville, Ohio, which has met monthly since 1984.

Steve Van Allen, retired, works part time at the Cincinnati Art Museum. He was employed by the U.S. Dept. of State from 1998 to 2005, and lived in Chennai, India and Gabon, West Africa, Argentine, and other countries, with Belize being his favorite. He earned his B.A. in photography with a minor in English, focusing on Shakespeare and modern poetry, from Ohio State University. A constant student, haiku is his favorite art form. He also plays the ukulele.

Contributor Biographies

MJ Werthman White has published poetry in *The Dayton Daily* News, *The Yellow Springs News*, and in local and national journals. In 2006 she was awarded the Paul Laurence Dunbar Poetry Prize. Billy Collins chose one of her poems as the adult winner of a Borders' 2009 national on-line poetry contest. In 2012, she was the recipient of the Antioch Writers' Workshop's Judson Jerome poetry award and scholarship. Her poetry collection, *How the Universe says Yes to Me,* was published in April 2017. Her poems can be heard on *Conrad's Corner* on public radio station WYSO.